I'm Reading About

TENNESSEE

The Volunteer State!

GALLOPADE

by Carole Marsh

Printed and Manufactured in Peachtree City, GA., USA
www.gallopade.com

Book design: John Hanson

Editorial manager: Janice Baker

Tennessee is a great state.

It is one of a kind.

What makes Tennessee special?

Let's read about it

and see!

NATIVE AMERICANS

Who lived in Tennessee first?

Native Americans did!

They moved around to find food.
They hunted in Tennessee's woods.
They fished in Tennessee's rivers.
They gathered fruits and seeds and nuts.

EXPLORERS

The first explorers came to Tennessee in 1540.
They came from the country of Spain.

Hernando de Soto was their leader.
He and his men were looking for cities of gold!

SETTLEMENT

A man named William Bean
came to Tennessee from Virginia.
He was looking for a new place to hunt and live.
He started a settlement on the Watauga River.

William Bean's family became
known as the
"First Family of Tennessee."

Watauga River
Watauga River

STATEHOOD

Tennessee was the 16th state to join the United States of America!

Isn't it great,
to be a state!
I bet Tennessee
could hardly wait!

Tennessee became a state in 1796.

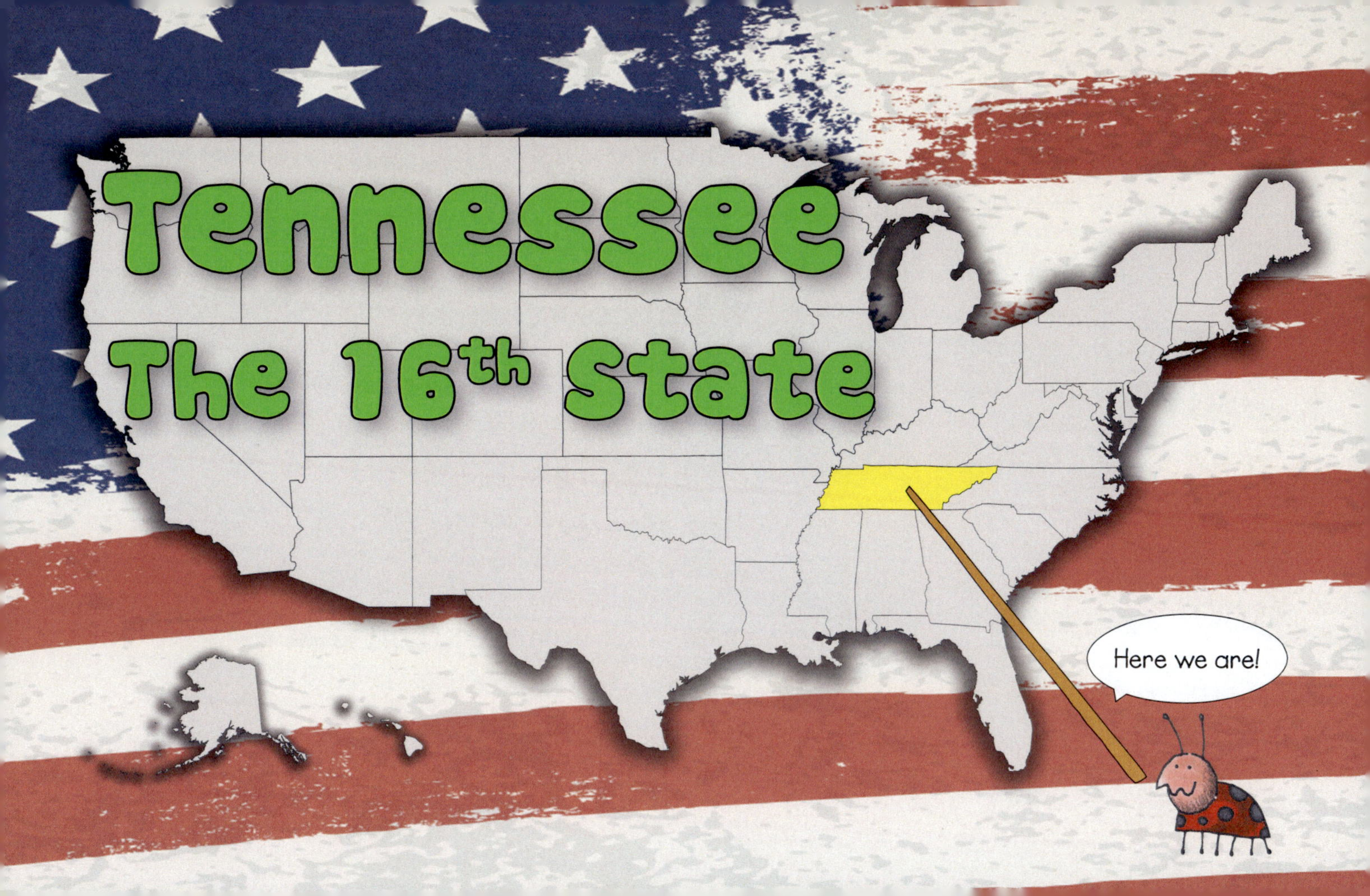
Tennessee
The 16th State
Here we are!

FLAG

I am the state flag.
I was adopted in 1905.

What colors am I?
Red. White. Blue.

Look at me.
What else do you see?

I fly high over the state of Tennessee!

CAPITAL

Say hello to Nashville,
the capital city of Tennessee!

There is an important building in Nashville.
It is the State Capitol.
Tennessee's laws are made there!

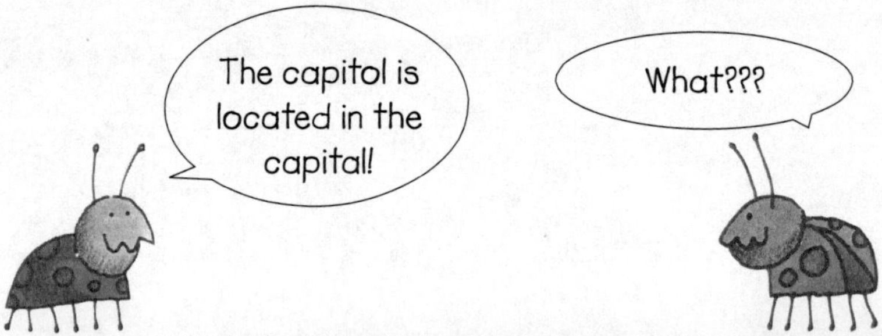

Capitol
Nashville
Capital

SEAL

I am a seal,
but I am not the State Seal.
If I were, I would be very important.
I would be stamped on many official papers.
(Ouch, that might hurt!)

THE GREAT SEAL OF THE STATE OF TENNESSEE
XVI
AGRICULTURE
COMMERCE
1796
Now, that's official!

NICKNAME

State nicknames are fun!
State nicknames are great!
They share fun facts
about each state!

Tennessee's nickname is "The Volunteer State."

Many Tennessee soldiers volunteered
to serve during times of war.
That's how Tennessee got its nickname.

The Volunteer State

BORDERS

Look at Tennessee.
Tennessee is in a region called "the South."

Tennessee borders eight other states.
Find them on the map!

Tennessee came from the Native American word *Tanasi.*

Borders

VIRGINIA
KENTUCKY
MISSOURI
NORTH CAROLINA
TENNESSEE
ARKANSAS
MISSISSIPPI
ALABAMA
GEORGIA
ATLANTIC OCEAN
Howdy, neighbors!

PRESIDENT

The President is the leader of our country.
He lives in Washington, D.C.
That is the capital of the United States.

The President lives in a big house
called the White House.

Several United States Presidents lived in Tennessee!

Andrew Jackson
7th President
James K. Polk
11th President
Andrew Johnson
17th President

PEOPLE

Many famous people

Sequoyah

Created method so Cherokee people could read and write

Davy Crockett

Frontiersman called "King of the Wild Frontier"

Hattie Caraway

First woman elected to the U.S. Senate

call our state home!

Let's hang out!

Wilma Rudolph

First U.S. woman to win three gold medals at one Olympics

Elvis Presley

Singer known as the "King of Rock and Roll"

Albert Gore Jr.

45th Vice President of the United States

PEOPLE

Mockingbird

I am the state bird, and I fly
over Tennessee, proud and high.

As I fly, up in the sky,
I flap my wings to tell you "Hi!"

The Tennessee state bird is the Mockingbird.

BIRD

Iris

FLOWER

I am the Iris.
I am the state flower.

I grow where it's warm and sunny.
I bloom in spring and summer.
I help make Tennessee beautiful!

Look at me! Smell me!
I grow on a long green stem!

Tulip Poplar

TREE

I am a Tulip Poplar—I'm the state tree.
All over Tennessee is where to find me.

My roots run deep, they keep me strong.
I can live for hundreds of years—that's very long!

I stand up straight, big and tall.
Don't climb too high—it would hurt to fall!

Ladybug

INSECT

I am the Ladybug.
I am one of the state insects.

I am a type of beetle.
I am red with black polka dots!

Gardeners and farmers love me.
I eat bugs off their plants.
I help Tennessee crops grow.

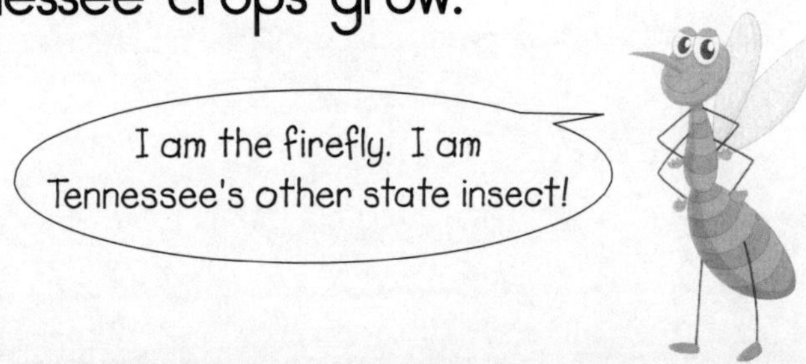

Tennessee Caves

CAVES

Let's explore Tennessee's caves!

Tennessee has many caves.
They are cool and dark and wet.
Some even have waterfalls and lakes!

Tennessee's caves are home to many animals:

Bats **Spiders** **Cave Salamanders** **Cave Crickets**

The Great Smoky Mountains

MOUNTAINS

Tennessee's Smoky Mountains are the place to be.
Hiking, fishing, camping—
fun for you and me.

If you were to climb
to the top of a tree,
you might see clear across Tennessee!

Tennessee River

RIVERS

Tennessee has many rivers.
People like to use them
for boating and fishing!

This habitat is home to many animals:

Birds **Deer** **Snakes** **Frogs** **Fish** **and More!**

River otters live in
Tennessee's rivers.
They are very smart animals.
They love to play, too!

Graceland

LANDMARK

Graceland is a beautiful mansion!
The famous singer, Elvis Presley, lived there.
Graceland is in Memphis.

Many people visit Graceland each year.
They walk around the home to see how Elvis lived.

Tennessee Crops

Tennessee has many farms.
Why?
Because Tennessee has good soil and a warm climate!

Some of the top crops grown in Tennessee include:

Soybeans **Cotton**

Corn **Tobacco**

Hey!
Don't forget about me!
I am a cow from Tennessee.
Tennessee farms raise lots of cows!

Mooooooo!

Sports in Tennessee

SPORTS

Baseball! Basketball! Football!
Tennessee has it all.

Whether you like to watch or play,
You are sure to have a ball!

Titans Volunteers Tigers

Commodores

& More!

Tennessee: Home of Music City

CLAIM TO FAME

Nashville is called "Music City"!
It is the home of country music.
Many famous musicians and songwriters live and work there.

The Country Music Hall of Fame is in Nashville.

Missouri is a great state.
It is one of a kind.

What makes Missouri special?
Let's read about it
and see!

NATIVE AMERICANS

Who lived in Missouri first?

Native Americans did!

They moved around to find food.
They hunted in Missouri's woods.
They fished in Missouri's rivers.
They gathered fruits and seeds and nuts.

EXPLORERS

The first explorers came to Missouri in 1673.
They came from the country of France.

Father Jacques Marquette and Louis Joliet
were their leaders.
They were exploring the Mississippi River!

SETTLEMENT

New settlers came to Missouri in the early 1700s.
They started a settlement in Missouri.
They named it Ste. Genevieve.

Settlers in Ste. Genevieve grew wheat, tobacco, maize, and other crops.

Ste. Genevieve
Ste.
Genevieve

STATEHOOD

Missouri was the 24th state
to join the United States of America!

Isn't it great,
to be a state!
I bet Missouri
could hardly wait!

Missouri became a state in 1821.

Missouri
The 24th State
Here we are!

FLAG

I am the state flag.
I was adopted in 1913.

What colors am I?
Red. White. Blue.

Count my stars.
Count my stripes.

Look at me.
What else do you see?

UNITED WE STAND DIVIDED WE FALL
SALUS
POPULI SUPREMA
LEX ESTO
MDCCCXX

CAPITAL

Say hello to Jefferson City,
the capital city of Missouri!

There is an important building in Jefferson City.
It is the State Capitol.
Missouri's laws are made there!

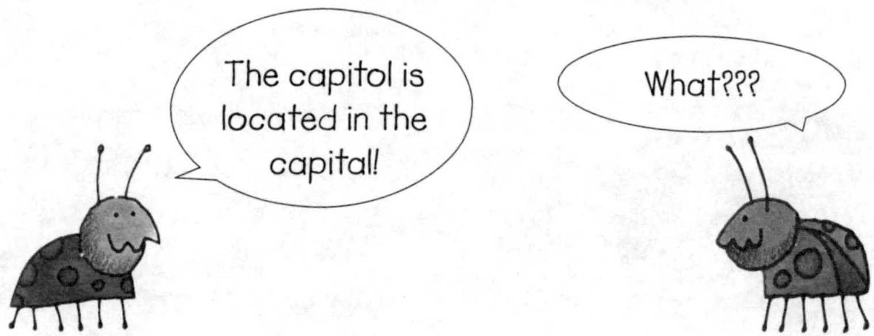

Capitol
Capital
Jefferson City

SEAL

I am a seal,
but I am not the State Seal.
If I were, I would be very important.
I would be stamped on many official papers.
(Ouch, that might hurt!)

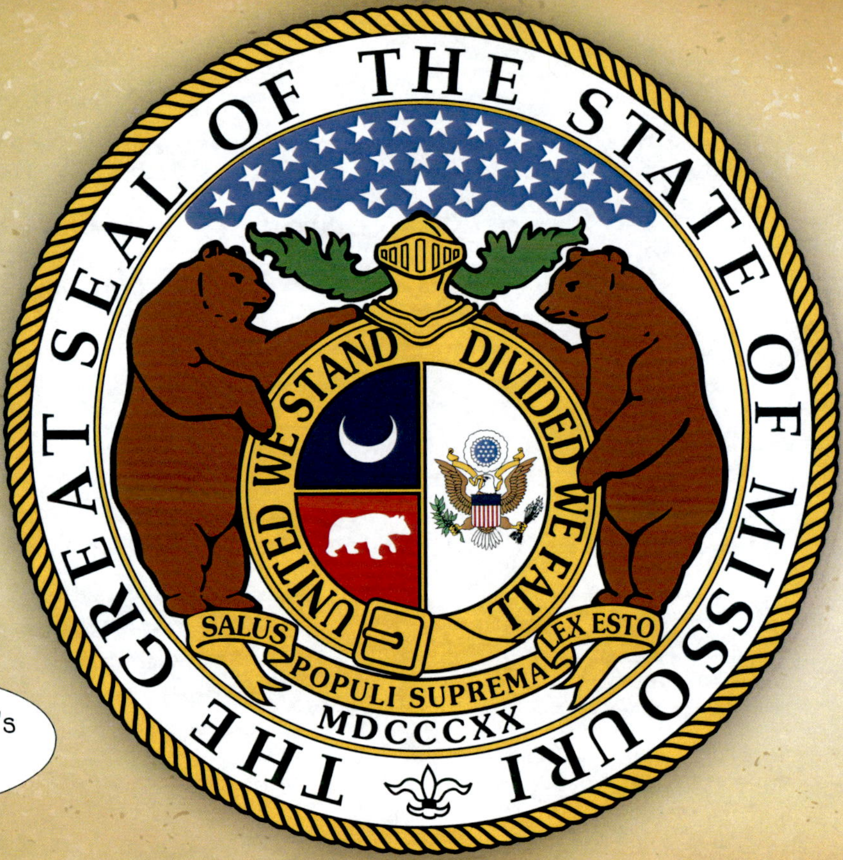
THE GREAT SEAL OF THE STATE OF MISSOURI
UNITED WE STAND DIVIDED WE FALL
SALUS POPULI SUPREMA LEX ESTO
MDCCCXX

Now, that's official!

NICKNAME

State nicknames are fun!
State nicknames are great!
They share fun facts
about each state!

Missouri's nickname is "The Show Me State."

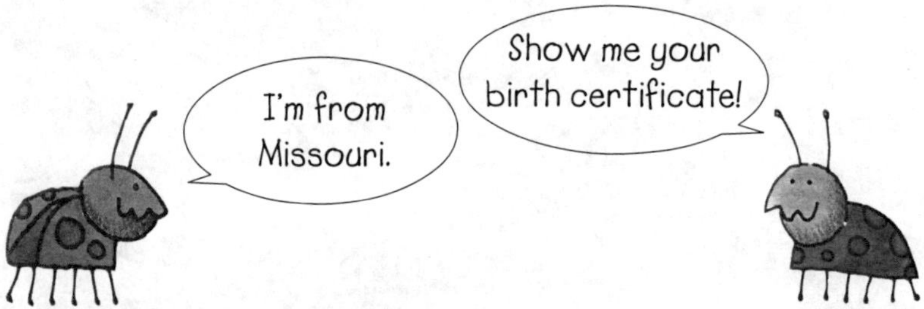

The Show Me State

BORDERS

Look at Missouri.
Missouri is in a region called "the Midwest."

Missouri borders eight other states.
Find them on the map!

Missouri comes from an Indian word that means "town of large canoes."

Borders

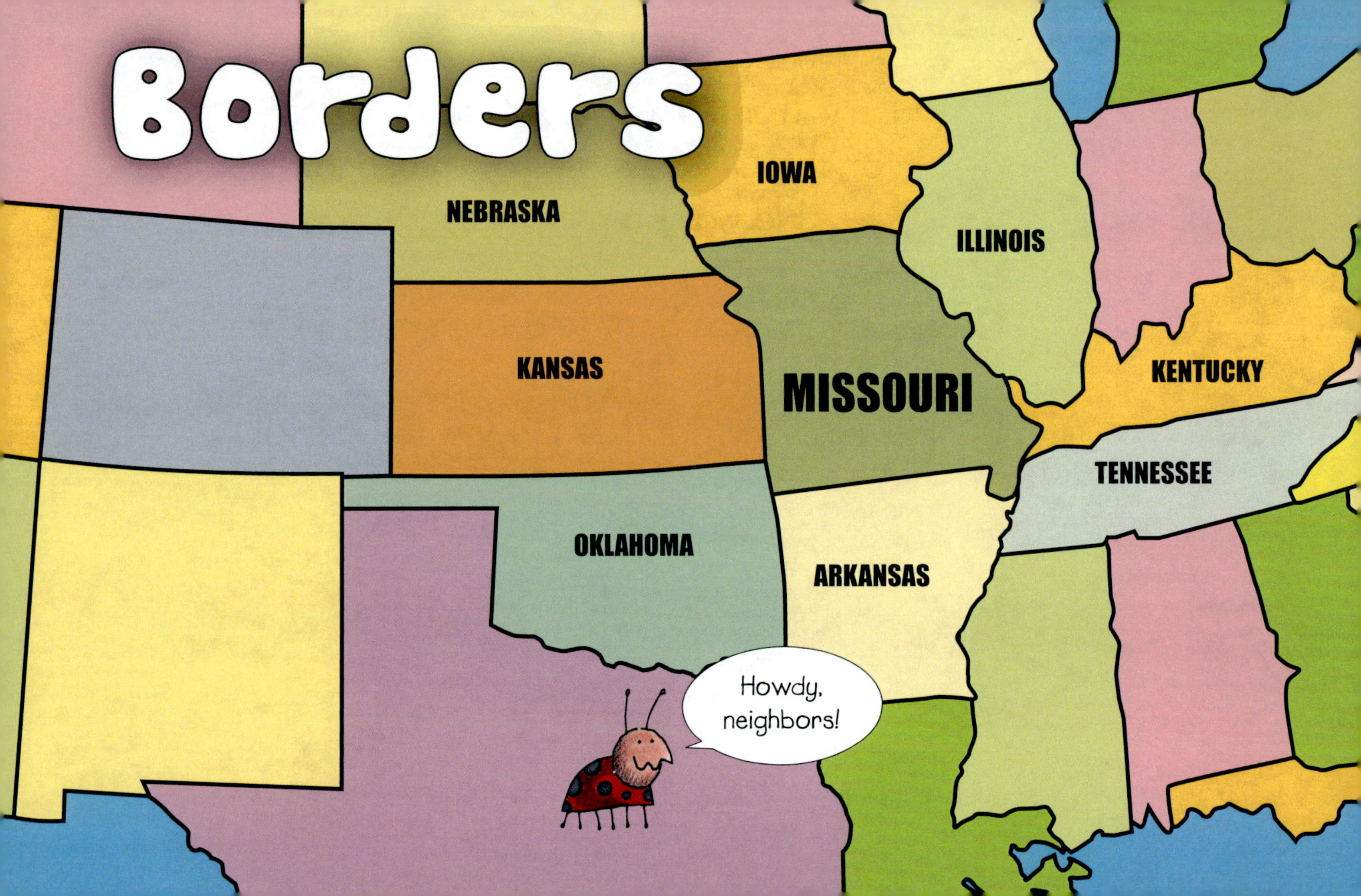
NEBRASKA
IOWA
ILLINOIS
KANSAS
MISSOURI
KENTUCKY
TENNESSEE
OKLAHOMA
ARKANSAS
Howdy, neighbors!

PRESIDENT

Harry Truman was the 33rd President
of the United States of America.
He was born in Missouri!

Harry Truman was born in a town called Lamar.
He liked to read.
He was very good at playing the piano!

Harry Truman

Many famous people

Daniel Boone

Explorer and frontiersman

Samuel Clemens (Mark Twain)

One of America's greatest writers

George Washington Carver

Scientist who greatly improved farming in the South

call our state home!

Let's hang out!

Laura Ingalls Wilder

Author of *Little House* series of children's books

James Cash (J.C.) Penney

Founded J.C. Penney stores

Walt Disney

Created Mickey Mouse, Disneyland, and Walt Disney World

PEOPLE

Bluebird

BIRD

I am the state bird, and I fly
over Missouri, proud and high.

As I fly, up in the sky,
I flap my wings to tell you "Hi!"

The Missouri state bird is the Bluebird.

White Hawthorn Blossom

I am the White Hawthorn Blossom.
I am the state flower.

I grow where it's warm and sunny.
I bloom in early spring.
I help make Missouri beautiful!

Look at me! Smell me!
I bloom on the Hawthorn Tree!

FLOWER

Flowering Dogwood

TREE

I am a Flowering Dogwood—I'm the state tree.
All over Missouri is where to find me.

My roots run deep, they keep me strong.
I can live for about 80 years—that's very long!

I stand up straight, big and tall.
Don't climb too high—it would hurt to fall!

Honeybee

INSECT

I am the Honeybee.
I am the state insect.

I might sting you if you bother me,
But really, I am your friend.

I carry pollen from flower to flower.
I make honey.
I help Missouri crops grow.

BZZZZZZZZZZZ!

Caves

Let's explore Missouri's caves!

Missouri has many caves.
They are cool and dark and wet.
Some even have waterfalls
and lakes!

Missouri's caves are home to many animals:

Bats

Spiders

Cave Salamanders

Cave Crickets

CAVES

Mountains

MOUNTAINS

Missouri's mountains are the place to be.
Hiking, fishing, camping—
fun for you and me.

If you were to climb
to the top of a tree,
you'd have a very nice view to see!

Rivers

RIVERS

Missouri has many rivers!
Early settlers built towns along Missouri's rivers.
They traveled along the rivers on flatboats.

The river habitat is home to many animals:

Birds Deer Snakes Frogs Fish and More!

People enjoy all kinds of water sports on Missouri's rivers today!

Gateway Arch

LANDMARK

The Gateway Arch is a tall silver arch.
It is the tallest arch in the world!
It stands along the banks of the
Mississippi River in St. Louis.

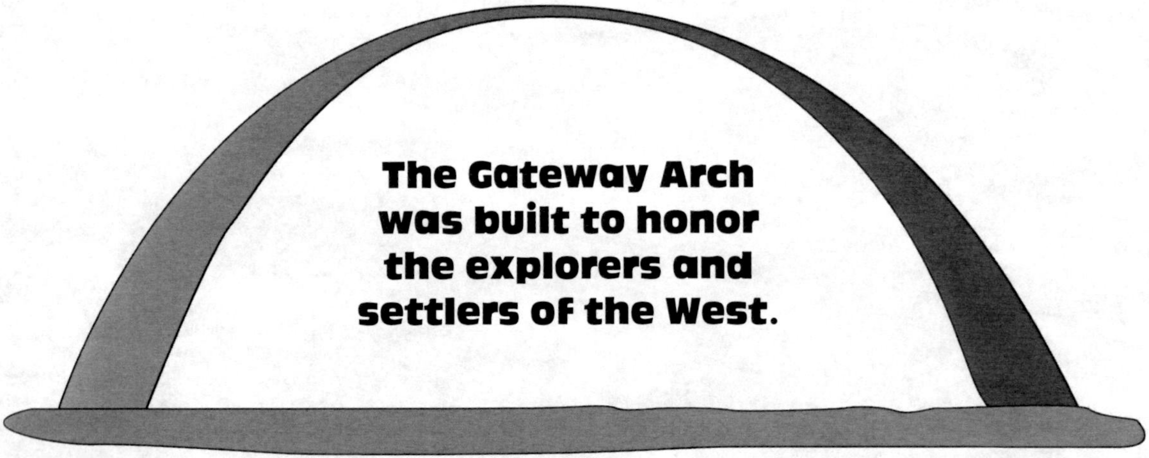

The Gateway Arch was built to honor the explorers and settlers of the West.

Missouri Crops

Missouri has many farms.
Why?
Because Missouri has good soil and a mild climate!

Some of the top crops grown in Missouri are:

Soybeans **Corn** **Hay** **Cotton**

Sports in Missouri

SPORTS

Baseball! Basketball! Football!
Missouri has it all.

Whether you like to watch or play,
You are sure to have a ball!

Chiefs **Rams** **Cardinals**

Royals

Tigers

Bears

& More!

St. Louis: Gateway to the West

CLAIM TO FAME

St. Louis, Missouri, is called the
Gateway to the West!

The explorers Lewis and Clark started their journey in St. Louis.
They traveled west along the Missouri River.
They were the first Americans to explore the western United States.

Many settlers passed through St. Louis on their way west.

GLOSSARY

birth certificate: an official document that proves where a person was born

climate: weather conditions in an area over a long period of time

elect: to choose someone by voting

flatboat: a boat with a flat bottom and square ends used to carry goods and people on rivers

gateway: a point where a place or region may be entered

habitat: a place where plants or animals naturally live

laws: rules made by the government

pollen: a yellow powder that helps plants make new plants

region: an area that has similar characteristics

settlement: the first community in an area

GLOSSARY

climate: weather conditions in an area over a long period of time

elect: to choose someone by voting

frontiersman: a person who lives on new, unsettled land

habitat: a place where plants or animals naturally live

laws: rules made by the government

mansion: a large, impressive house

musician: a person who plays a musical instrument

region: an area that has similar characteristics

settlement: the first community in an area

volunteer: a person who offers to do a service without being asked or assigned to do it